Honor Society Professional Network Guide

How to Build Your Personal Brand

Brittany Moradian, Mike Moradian

CONTENTS

Introduction

Thanks to social media, readily available technology, and smartphones in our pockets, personal branding has never been more important. You are a brand, whether you want to embrace it or not. As a brand, people are consuming you, your content, and your message on a daily basis. Choosing to leverage that brand for your own personal and professional advancement is one of the smartest things you could be doing today, which is why we want to explore the nuances of creating an advantageous brand, made just for you.

According to a CareerBuilder survey, 70% of employers use social media to screen candidates before selecting them for a position. This should tell you that the pictures, posts, and shared articles on your feeds are much more important than you might think – they could make or break your future. When these employers stumble on your social media profiles, what do they see? A cohesive brand that makes them want to work with you, or a jumbled mix of on-topic or inappropriate posts that indicate you aren't ready for the job yet?

What is a Personal Brand?

A personal brand is the culmination of your online presence; yet, it's so much more than that. A strong brand stands out against the crowd. When you walk into a sporting goods store, do you walk over to the Nike Swoosh, or to the brand you've never heard of? We are more inclined to trust a known, solidified brand than one that appears to be disjointed and disorganized. A good brand translates to more sales, increased awareness, and a better customer experience.

This branding isn't just reserved for companies anymore. It's reserved for you and freely available to anyone who wants to get up and create a personal brand that is supportive of their future.

Your personal brand is who you are, what you stand for, the values you embrace, and the way in which you choose to express these values. A brand is a quick culmination of your identity and clear value, for employers, friends, partners, and even mates to observe. It's presenting your own personal story – how are you telling it? The good news is, you are in complete control of how this story is told! It's a story that can establish and boost your career more than anything else today.

As Forbes famously said, *"Why Personal Branding is More Important Than Ever: Whether you're an employee or entrepreneur, cultivating a personal brand has become more important than ever before."*

Personal branding can no longer be ignored. An overwhelming 85% of hiring managers report that a job candidate's personal brand influences their hiring decision. In this book, we are going to explore the concept of a personal brand, how to grow your brand, and how to set the foundation for a professional life that is going to carry you through your goals. Here at HonorSociety.org, we are passionate about helping current students, graduates, or possible-students to pursue their professional and educational dreams. Knowledge is power, which is why we want to help all readers enrich their knowledge of personal branding today.

About the Authors

Mike Moradian.

Mike is the executive director of Honor Society, as well as the author of the "HonorSociety.org Strength & Honor" series. He is also the founder of CampusBuddy and CollegeBudget.

On a mission to empower and equip students with everything they need to be successful today and, in the future, Mike is constantly learning about new education and career trends he can share with Honor Society members. Mike understands how important prior preparation can be for a successful job-search out of college, which is why he is constantly authoring new books that uncover every last bit of detail for students.

No stranger to the world of recruiting, education, and job searching, Mike has been in the business for over 10-years to date. In 2010, Mike was named to the Bloomberg Businessweek's America's Best Young Entrepreneur's List. Two years later, Mike was the youngest executive to be named to the "top 40 under 40" by Direct Marketing News. Lastly, Mike was also showcased in a US Embassy publication entitled, "Why Did You Become an Entrepreneur?" He was subsequently recognized at the White House as an award recipient recognizing young entrepreneurship.

In *How to Search for Your Career Online*, Mike is working to further his available educational resources for Honor Society members, uncovering some of the best advice for students looking to hone in on their career search. It is recommended that readers also consider downloading Moradian's *"How to Build Your Personal Brand"* book, which goes hand-in-hand with this guide.

Brittany Moradian

Brittany is a Scholarships Program Director at the Honor Society Foundation. She focuses on the development of scholarship programs at our incredible foundation, as well as the advancement of programming around foundation's philanthropic missions, core values, and leadership initiatives.

She felt called to co-write this book for all individuals struggling to approach the concept of personal branding. As she watched this concept become more and more important today, she want to ensure she have done everything in her power to equip people moving forward. If you have any questions at the end of this book, please do not hesitate to reach out to Brittany or our foundation.

Thank you.

CHAPTER 1

Get to Know Yourself

As Aristotle famously said: "Knowing yourself is the beginning of all wisdom."

If you want to build a personal brand that works for you and your dreams, you need to first know who you are. This can be a difficult and uncomfortable conversation to have with ourselves, since many of us try and "rebrand" ourselves as someone else throughout our lives. It's important to remember there is only one you in the world, and that's something to embrace.

We all have strengths and weaknesses. Trying to bury or ignore the weaknesses will make you weaker in the end. Rather, get to know yourself, what you are good at, what you are bad at, and what you like to do with your time. Here are some questions you can ask yourself:

- What motivates me?
- What drains my energy?
- What do I have a hard time doing?
- What kind of work am I good at?

- What kind of work am I bad at?

- What kind of projects take me way too long to complete?

- What are my passions?

If it's hard for you to answer these questions, ask your closest friends and family what they would say. Sometimes, a third-party perspective can help us see ourselves with more clarity. We can build up mental roadblocks or barriers over time when in reality, we fail to realize what actually makes us happy.

What Are Your Values and Passions?

Your values are the things that you believe to be important in your life. They are at the core of who you are and what you prioritize on a daily basis. This can include honesty, loyalty, family, selflessness, community, etc. When it comes down to hard decisions and adversity, we always fall back on our values to get us through it.

These values become relevant in the job searching process. If a candidate's values line up with that of the company's, they are more likely to reach out to you and hire you. Best of all, you'll be happier in a job that has the same values as you! Communicating these values clearly through your personal brand will set you up for a productive and fulfilling career.

And what about your passions? What do you do to pass the time when no is looking? Do you swim, draw, paint, cook, clean, etc.? As for your professional passions, do you like automation, social media, photography, or organizing? We all have different passions, and those passions light a fire in our soul. If we live a life in which we are unable to devote any time to these passions, our happiness and contentment will decrease. As this happens, it will make us feel lost and ill-placed at our jobs. Therefore, be public in your expression of your passions – take classes and do what you want to do to explore your natural likes.

Together, values and passions will help you determine where you want to be today, tomorrow, and 10-years from now. The ideal career path will form and you won't even need to do anything about – recruiters will see your brand and just know you are the right pick.

Your Key Traits

What makes you unique? What helps you stand out from the crowd? Here are the Big Five Personality Traits:

- Openness to new things
- Conscientiousness
- Extraversion
- Agreeableness
- Neuroticism

Do you lean more towards neuroticism and less towards extraversion? There is no one "right way" to approach these five traits. But, being aware of them can help you harness your uniqueness in your branding. If you accept that you are incredibly conscientious and not at all extraverted, own that in your content and branding. We all have strengths and weaknesses – no humans are immune to weakness.

Embrace the Niche

With so many people online today, it's important to embrace the concept of niche marketing. This is a form of marketing in which you pick a specific niche and stick to it with all of your branding. Although you may feel the pull to pursue a "catch-all" form of branding that you feel will appeal to everyone, this can actually narrow your chances by making you too generic. Your personal brand is going to grow as you grow. You want to be known for yourself, your personality, and what makes you happy today. Pretending to like "everything" may cause recruiters to approach you for jobs that will not bring you any personal contentment.

Choose Authenticity

The most important thing at the end of the day when it comes to building your personal brand is to choose authenticity. There is often times a misconception that building a personal brand means creating a character or persona. A persona is a façade, and it's now heading in the wrong direction from who you are as a person.

Going through our lists above, ask yourself the hard questions, write down your values and passions, figure out your key personality traits, and sit back and embrace it all. There is nothing you need to hide. Branding is not about positioning yourself as someone you are not. Rather, it's about strategically marketing who you ARE. Getting started with a personal brand begins with getting to know yourself. Take some time to journal, ask friends and family about your quirks and shortcomings, and pause to get to know yourself. This is a useful exercise for every single person on the planet – we could all spend more time getting to know ourselves!

CHAPTER 2

Identify Your Target Audience

Now that you've explored yourself, what makes you tick, and what makes you happy, it's time to think about your target audience. Who are you marketing to? What kind of companies do you want to approach you? What is your dream job and what companies provide this dream job? It's always important to think beyond yourself and consider the audience – the very people who are consuming the brand content.

As I hinted in the previous chapter, one of the biggest mistakes you can make with a personal brand is trying to appeal to everyone. Not everyone is going to be your "ideal" client. In fact, wasting time on people who do not have your dream job at the other end is only going to detract from the time you could have been spending to enrich your future.

In order to find the right companies, jobs, and partners, you need to be willing to say no to the ones that aren't right for you. This means that you need to identify a specific target audience and build a brand that is going to resonate with them.

Don't let this confuse you into thinking you need to make a persona. Rather, you need to harness your brand, yourself, and your quirks, and what kind of content you can make with your personality that these audience members are going to like.

The best way to get started with this is a little exercise: creating your dream client (job offering).

Your Dream Job/Career

If I sat you down right now and told you that you could have any job in the world, what would your answer be? Think about that job, the companies that offer that job, and the people that work at that job. You really want to explore the details of it so that you can better understand your audience.

Let's say you want to be an editor at a fashion magazine in New York City. What do those current editors do right now? What does their social media look like? Do they spend time writing their think pieces and positioning themselves as thought leaders? Do they have their own blogs where they share their personal fashion? Do your homework and learn more about the content they are producing.

It's not always roses, either. What do you think are the challenges in this position? Probably work–life balance, right?

Dive deeper and consider the following details:

- Demographics: what is the average age, relationship status, income, etc. for this role?

- Desires and aspirations: what do a fashion editors desire for their future? To own the fashion magazine?
- Challenges: what do editors struggle with – can you handle those struggles?

Take time to research this profile so you can sit back and understand if that's the profile you want for yourself. If you notice that the current editors put a ton of time into their own personal blog, then consider launching your own personal blog as part of your brand. Continue to be yourself and share content related to what makes you happy, of course, but format it and bundle it up in a way that is going to resonate with your audience.

Always consider who you are trying to reach with your brand. If you are going after a more millennial job, then your social media presence is going to be paramount. However, if you want to join a skills trade and get down and dirty with your hands, then you may want to consider the importance of professional groups and local networking. It's all about understanding where your audience resides.

In the coming chapters, we are going to look at the specifics of how to build a tangible personal brand that is right for your interests. We're going to look at your online presence, personal image, and physical assets, like business cards, as well as following the experts, and most importantly, engaging in networking.

Are you ready to get started?

CHAPTER 3

Online Presence

Almost <u>4.57 billion people</u> were active on the internet as of July 2020, which includes 59% of the entire world population. We are all using the internet like never before, especially during coronavirus, to connect, share, comment, apply for jobs, and bond with new people. The internet has transcended simply being helpful for sharing photos, and has become integral to just about everything we do today.

Therefore, your online presence and how you choose to present yourself to the world is incredibly valuable. It can make or break your future, your potential, and your job prospects. As I mentioned earlier, almost three-fourths of companies are looking at your social media profiles before they choose to bring you in for a second interview. What do they see when they take in your online presence?

Naturally, there are a lot of places to provide your content today. How do you choose which social media apps to use? You can't possibly make content for 15 different sites, per day, right? That is correct. You don't want to dilute yourself or your brand – your content will become less authentic and engaging.

Your online presence is going to look different depending on which mediums you choose. However, we are going to recommend three essential places to be sharing content and reaffirming your professional today:

LinkedIn

Known as the "professional networking social media platform," LinkedIn has solidified itself as the go-to place for making yourself a professional. It's the ultimate site for defining your brand as a serious, working adult. You can network in groups, share posts, publish your own LinkedIn articles, and bolster up your profile to be a living, breathing resume. What are some other ways to ensure your LinkedIn is converting for you, every time?

- **Your Skills:** What are the industry skills needed for your future job? Recruiters will often use LinkedIn with a keyword search for skills required for their job. It's important to feature industry terms in your profile, including the headline, summary, and job descriptions. If you want that job as a fashion editor, then they are going to be looking up: editor, fashion, managing editor, journalist, fashion journalist, etc. Be sure your profile is filled with the right keywords.

- **The Data:** If you can provide some quantification at times, it's going to bode well for you. How many projects have you completed to date? How many articles? Provide some actual data and empirical evidence on your profile that can help a recruiter get a feel for how serious and eager to work you are.

- **Comprehensiveness:** LinkedIn allows you to put a ton of stuff on your profile. From a summary and past job experiences, to linked article features, published articles, endorsements, hobbies, and more, don't leave any stones unturned. If you leave part of your profile blank, it will communicate an unwillingness to follow through. Convince them that you are the person they should hire.

- **Crisp Imagery:** Please, do not use an unprofessional or blurry photo as your LinkedIn profile picture. Use a professionally shot portrait. This can be done in any local photography studio. It will immediately tell the profile viewer that you are serious and you mean business.

- **Thought Leadership:** Even if you're not a good writer, it's worth writing LinkedIn Articles in your industry niche. You can always hire freelance editors to clean up the article before you publish it. These articles make you look like an expert and someone who is passionate about your industry. It also shows you're not afraid to put in the extra work and go above and beyond.

- **Giving Back:** Recruiters want to see some personality and that you spend your time doing things that enrich the community around you. By being part of our Honor Society, you can add your participating in our community as part of your profile. An honor society accreditation implies you are hardworking, smart, and willing to volunteer. Truly, you can never have enough community-oriented attributes on your LinkedIn profile.

Note: Be sure to update your LinkedIn monthly. Many times, people will ignore their LinkedIn for months while big changes occur in their professional lives.

Twitter

Twitter is a great social media platform for highlighting and building upon your industry expertise. Instead of using the app for trolling people and firing out insults at past coworkers, why not use Twitter to your advantage? Try to incorporate your personal brand into your Twitter bio by using those key hashtags again. Look them up and follow others in your space that you aspire to be like – what kind of bio do they have? What kind of hashtags to they use?

Remember that every tweet is a part of your professional image. Would you feel comfortable if your boss read every tweet on your profile? If not, consider cleaning it up and deleting any negative tweets that show a different side to you.

Additional Twitter tips:

- **The Cover Image:** Consider using a freelancing site to have a cover image made for your Twitter profile. It can be a picture of you formatted with your tagline or your passions. If not, use a blank color or a professional photo that is crisp and clear.

- **Tweet Often:** Tweeting is easy and can be done in seconds. Take time to tweet every day about something in your industry. Even if it's just retweeting another article, this will tell recruiters you are passionate about your industry and actively engaged in reading about it.

- **Follow Experts:** Twitter is a great place to follow the experts in your industry. See what they are tweeting about. What are the latest trends or considerations? You can learn about it first on Twitter and head over to LinkedIn where you can write about it.

- **The Bio Link:** Twitter allows you to link to one website in your bio. Where should that link to? Your personal website, of course!

Your Website

A major component of building an online presence and brand is having your own personal website. Websites aren't just for clothing stores and blogs anymore – they are a great way to solidify your brand, grow your prospects, and feature your accomplishments.

Where do you get started with having your own website? For starters, you can create one on: Squarespace, Wix, or WordPress.

Many come with a few free templates you can use to build the site. Membership costs are usually $8 to $12 per month. The sites will bring you through a step-by-step building process to ensure all of the information is filled out.

You can also use helpful resources like Canva and Venngage's logo templates to get started with your graphic elements. Be sure to pick two to three colors that you use with everything. This will help recruiters get a feel for your "brand" that they can reference at a later date.

Additional tips when making your own personal website:

- **Keep it Simple:** No one wants to sift through essays and confusing interfaces on a website. Keep it light, brief, and easy to follow. Use white as your main website color and allow the few spots of text to speak for themselves.

- **Rely on Imagery:** Humans are highly visual creatures. That's why pictures improve website conversion rates by 65%. It's easier for us to feel connected to someone through a photo than it is a paragraph. These photos will make it easy for recruiters to see you, and really, get to know you through your website. Don't shy away from plenty of bright, crisp imagery.

- **Back Up Your Expertise:** Reaffirm your expertise in an industry by linking to your press coverage. If you don't have any, consider writing and sending out a press release about yourself to news outlets you can post to the site. Additionally, write your own articles and add a blog tab to the website. This is where you can show-off your industry passion and knowledge.

- **Keep it Modest:** It's always good to flaunt it, but within reason. Don't make the website one big obsession pulpit for you and your accomplishments. Instead, make it more so about how you can help other people and impact your industry with what you've done and accomplished so far. Shift the spotlight off of yourself so the website is more approachable.

What should appear on my home page?

If you're not a web designer, you are probably wondering what exactly should appear on your home page. Here are some key elements that will make your brand irresistible to those dropping by:

- **A Professional Logo:** Since this is a personal brand, it can merely be your name in a special cursive font. You can also consider a logo related to a brand that you market yourself behind. Let's say you're passionate about sustainable thrifting. You may have a brand, "The Thrifted Closet" that you brand synonymously with yourself. There's no harm in having a logo made for that!

- **Your Value Proposition:** You need to be able to communicate, in one sentence, who you help, how you help them, and what makes you unique. This should be near the top of the page.

- **Images of YOU:** Forget the stock images, no one wants to see them. Provide imagery of you throughout the page.

- **Social Proof:** Feature a feed of your recent social media posts to highlight your activity in the industry.

- **Call-to-Action**: Give the website visitor a clear next step. "Click here" to learn more about a blog, article, availability, etc. This will implore the website visitors to give you a call about a potential job opening.

What About Other Social Media Sites?

We can't forget about Facebook, Instagram, and TikTok. All of the same rules go for these sites: post professional content, use the same colors if possible, and position yourself as someone who is passionate about your industry. Remember that every social media profile you have is fair game to a recruiter, which is why you will want to consider making them private if you are not putting your usual branding effort into their presentation. But, if you are going to take your time with these sites and make them part of your story, then they can certainly augment your online presence.

Honor Society Vanity URL

Here at Honor Society, we understand the importance of an online presence, which is why we provide all members with a descriptive profile and vanity URL. It's an easy way to extend the professionalism of your online image, as well as communicate what you are serious about. If you want to check out an example, click the link here: https://www.honorsociety.org/members/mike-moradian.

Next, let's look at the details related to your own personal, physical image.

CHAPTER 4

Your Personal Image

Remember when I said that your visual presentation is much more important than your writing-based presentation? I am going to explore in-depth what I meant by that in this chapter.

The nature of the online world is a visual one today. Many of these people have never – and will never – meet you in person. They have to go off of the content they find online. At the end of the day, we connect with other people when we look them in the eye, shake their hands, hug them, and speak with them. To be human is to connect to the people around us. With the online world, we are missing out on some of that innate connection, which is why visuals have become so important. It's the next best thing.

Rewind back to your values, passions, and personality traits. One way to communicate them is through your personal image. It should complement everything you are already communicating with your social media and personal website. For some people, personal image can be a struggle – they don't like to spend time on themselves and their image. In this new world of personal branding, there's no room for imagery ignorance. That's what I am here to tell you.

So how do you ensure your personal image is in line with your online presence? Here are a few suggestions:

- **Your Headshots:** There is no replacement in the world for professional imagery and headshots. You can't take these with your phone and you can't have your parent take them with an old digital camera. You must work with a professional photographer with high quality equipment and studio lighting who can capture your essence and aura in a professional image. Consider having pictures taken in a few different outfits you can rotate around your social media profiles. Think back to your brand colors and try and bring them into these photos.

- **Your Article Covers:** Every time you post an article, a blog, etc., there is a photo that can go with that article. If possible, always try to make your image part of that cover. Have the professional photographer take pictures of you at your laptop or holding your phone. You can use these as part of your blog to really communicate your association with the information you are sharing. It's an easy way to add more imagery of yourself without seeming self-absorbed. You want recruiters to be able to identify your physical presentation.

- **Email Signature:** Don't just leave your name in texted font at the end of your email. Take the time to import your personal signature into your email. Include all of your contact information and your social media icons, as well. Make it easy for people to get to know you immediately. It's no time to be shy today.

- **Dress for Success:** Even if you're not going into an office right now, it's important to still dress for success. All of your social media photos should communicate your style and professionalism. How you choose to dress and present yourself immediately tells recruiters how serious you are about being a professional. They can tell through your social media, even in a COVID-19 world.

- **Grooming:** For men and women, updating your image with professional grooming, like haircuts, trims, etc. can go a long way. Showing employers that you're not afraid to go above and beyond with your image will speak volumes.

Updating Your Personal Image

No one wants to see photos of you from four-years ago. What do you look like right now? Be sure to update these photos regularly so that they are an accurate reflection of your real appearance. Recruiters will feel like you might be hiding something from them if your headshot is clearly a 10-year younger version of yourself. Of course, affording professional photography every year is not prudent. Therefore, I recommend having new headshots taken every three-years. This will keep your image transparent so people are more likely to trust you.

What if I am not happy with my current appearance?

Remember that your brand is supposed to be authentic YOU. There is nothing you need to do to alter your appearance. Rather, spend time updating your appearance to one that is professional and reflective of the job you want for yourself. Enhance your authentic self with clothing and pictures that are true to yourself.

Next, let's look at the value of physical branding assets, like business cards, regalia, certificates, and more.

CHAPTER 5

The Importance of Physical Branding

Despite the digital nature of our world and all of the online interactivity, there is still something to be said for physical assets. I'm talking about those business cards, certificates, graduation regalia, and other items that can back up the brand you've built for yourself. In this chapter, we're going to look at the importance of physical branding. As Entrepreneur.com famously published: "Business Cards Still Matter."

Why do business cards still matter? Let's look at a few reasons:

1. **Digital Information is Impersonal:** Certainly, brands everywhere are struggling to make a personal connection with customers in the age of digital. At the end of the day, looking into someone else's eyes is incomparable. Networking is all about making genuine connections, which can't happen with an email or a text. It can happen with a physical asset that you give to someone, almost like a present.

2. **Direct Marketing Still Works:** Email marketing, texts, and SEO require the receiver to click on something, open it, and digest the information. They aren't as effective, still, as in-

person greetings with a handshake and a business card. A business card doesn't depend on the other person downloading and reading something. It's a direct marketing information card that's already in their hand, sealed, and ready to go.

3. **Extension of Personal Brand:** A business card is a physical extension of your personal brand. In fact, it's the first impression of your personal brand. When you meet someone and hope they will call you, accept you into a program, or offer you a job, you want them to walk away with a good first impression, right? Your business card will do that for you. Merely having a business card to give away will impress many college recruiters as well.

4. **Sharing Afterwards:** When stellar business cards are placed into the hands of recruiters, hirers, and managers, they often times will share that card with other people at their company. Your phone number and email will make its rounds through the office as people share the information from person to person. It's much more likely to circulate your information than an email you send to a recruiter.

5. **Imply Preparedness:** At the end of the day, if you're a student, graduate student, or newly grad, your goal is to get a job, right? You want to show the recruiter that you are responsible and prepared. They want to know that you are going to do your work every day, responsibly, no questions

asked. A business card shows them you not only went out of your way to create a personal brand for yourself, but that you also invested your money into making business cards.

No matter how digital the world may become, some things will never replace the impressiveness of a business card.

The Presence of a Certificate

When you walk into an office and a see a big, impressive certificate framed and mounted on the wall, you immediately assume that person is legitimate, professional, and accomplished, right? A certificate communicates that person went above and beyond to complete something or attain an accreditation for themselves. They weren't content with being mediocre and mundane – they wanted to enhance their lives and really reach for the stars.

That's what a certificate can do in any office. We will issue a certificate to all Honor Society members that you can cherish and frame long after you are out of school. It's a great way to start off your career on the right foot with an impressive piece of paper that tells people you mean business.

What about a COVID-19 future when we aren't in an office?

As you know, Skyping and Zoom have become commonplace in the age of "new normal." We are all Zooming from our office spaces to look as professional as possible. Framing that certificate in the field of view for your video calls will give off the same kind of impressive professionalism as it would in person. People have two eyes – they can see what you are presenting to them. It's all about showing employers that aren't satisfied with less – you want more.

Honor Society Graduation Regalia

When it's time to walk across that stage and grab the diploma you worked so hard to achieve, you want to be decked out in all of your academic accomplishments. By becoming part of our honor society community, we will provide you with Honor Society Regalia you can wear in your graduation photos. We will also issue a member certificate that can be framed in any office setting. It's a great way to jumpstart your accreditations as a professional before you've even left the graduation stage.

CHAPTER 6

Follow the Experts

As a newly grad or student, you aren't quite an expert yet in your field, right? You need to follow the experts who inspired you to get involved with your industry in the first place. These are the thought leaders, the influencers, the researchers, and the public figures that represent where you want to be in 10 or 20-years with your career.

What do these people do every day? What do they publish? Do you read everything they release? You should! The information age has provided us with a never-ending slew of content that you can be consuming every single day, many times for free. You have nothing to lose by following the experts intently and absorbing every piece of information they are releasing to you.

Don't Just Follow Them – Invest in Them

I am suggesting that you go beyond just following these experts. Go online and find their:

- Blogs
- Profiles

- Contributor profiles

- Videos

- Social media profiles

Look for people who are successful in your field and examine what they are doing. Ask yourself these questions:

- What topics are they writing about?

- What trends are they writing about?

- What platforms are they using to disseminate their information?

- What are their recent projects? Who are they partnering with?

- Who are THEIR mentors? Who do these people look up to?

- Who are their friends? This is a great way to find even more experts to follow in your industry.

With this information, attempt to imitate them. I am not saying copy them or plagiarize them. Never do that. I am suggesting that you look for people who are successful and examine what they are doing. You will want to use their example for your life so you can start to position yourself as an expert in the same field.

Mentorship Arrangements

Many times, these experts will take on mentees that are eager to learn about them and their content. Be sure to look up any expert programs that are related to these experts. They may also host private Facebook or LinkedIn Groups whereby you can get even closer to them and their information. Everyone wants to give back when they get to the top – it may be easier than you think to get in closely with these people.

Remember: in building a personal brand, your goal is to stand out. You can't rise to the top without considering who is already at the top. It's merely doing your due diligence to study these people and see what they are doing/saying. Every single expert in the world had experts that came before them and inspired them.

CHAPTER 7

Professional Groups and Meetups

Once we get back to in-person gatherings and meetups, it will be time to hit the networking with extreme professionalism again. There is nothing that can substitute congregating in one space with a bunch of other people from your industry, all there looking to make connections and grow. It's a great setting in which you can enhance your personal brand and make connections that can win you entrance to the jobs of your dream, the programs of your dream, and the colleges of your dream.

After you've put in the work to define and present your personal brand, it's time to take that personal brand out in public. You want people to know your personal brand is there and it's serious, right? Here are a few places where you can introduce this seriousness to everyone else in your industry:

Networking Events (Local Industry Meetups)

Networking events are a great catch-all activity for people looking to make connections. Through Meetup.com and EventBrite.com, you can find plenty of free networking events in your area on a weekly basis. These events will be segmented out by type, size, and industry, so you can better refine that ones that are right for you and your goals. With just a few clicks, you can sign up for free and attend (some may require a $5 or $10 entrance depending upon drink and food availability).

When you finally arrive at these events, be sure to bring a few things with you:

- Your business cards. Now is the time to impress people with your preparedness, even if you're still enrolled in college.

- Your elevator pitch. We are going to look at this in the next chapter.

- Your authenticity: never go to a networking event and adopt this alternative persona that has nothing to do with your actual personality and likes.

- A crisp, clean professional appearance with clothing that is tailored to fit you perfectly. First impressions are lasting impressions.

- A bag of some sort that you can use to collect all of the business cards you are going to receive at the event.

Coming prepared to a networking event will help you stand out from the crowd. You want to be ready to take advantage of all of the amazing connections that are available in the room. The more you network at public meetups, the more likely you will be invited to more private, intimate networking events that require an invite. Make this one of your goals when you're first getting started.

Professional Groups

Moving past the public networking event is access to professional groups. These are smaller groups that are united around very niche topics related to your industry. In order to gain access to these groups, individuals have to go above and beyond in some capacity to sign up and apply. Here at Honor Society, we host our own professional group meetups that are restricted to our society members. This ensures that only professional, serious networking individuals are enabled to get in on the action. Your time is valuable, which is why we want to host events that will provide you with access to opportunity immediately.

We also proudly host banquets and member trips that provide a more intimate setting for our members:

- Our latest retreat with the Mayor of Los Angeles:
  https://www.youtube.com/watch?v=w5d3evYoziI.

- Our Washington D.C. trip that was provided for members:
  https://www.youtube.com/watch?v=r8qiDEsjisw.

We proudly host professional groups across the spectrum, as well as monthly events that will make it easier than ever before for you to advance your career. Don't forget to join the digital professional groups associated with these meetups, which can usually be found on

Facebook and LinkedIn. This is where some of the best offers and opportunities are provided.

Facebook Groups

Why should you consider joining a Facebook Group? One of the biggest reasons is to access the visibility that comes with these groups. On any given day, these groups can be buzzing with comments, breaking news, article shares, and more.

Many individuals will sign onto Facebook every day and engage with a couple groups where they can share their new articles and ideas. It kickstarts the conversation, as well as the engagement with the article for better algorithmic rankings.

Groups are more visible since the people who belong to the group receive notifications about new posts. This tends to keep the discussions going, especially since everyone in the group is united around a common passion.

In order to measure the effectiveness of a Facebook Group, consider a few items: active members, good descriptions, and low spam. If you don't like what you see, you are free to leave the group at any time!

Did you know: you can join up to 6,000 Facebook groups? It's time to get started!

If you really want to go above and beyond with impressing the members of your industry, consider making your own Facebook group! Let's say you want to work in digital marketing. Consider creating a group called: "Young Digital Marketers of the Future." Put time into creating the group rules, descriptions, and graphics. Once that's done, post it to your page and encourage people to join. Be sure to address pain points that make people more likely to join. You can mediate the group, check the fans, and access some of the best networking in the world. It will take some time, but it will certainly be worth it!

CHAPTER 8

Word of Mouth Marketing

For the final part of this book, I am going to look at the importance of word-of-mouth marketing and being able to confidently communicate who you are and what you do to strangers. Known as your "elevator pitch," you need to have this pitch refined, perfected, and ready to share at a moment's notice. Can you describe what you do, what your passions are, and really, who you are? Can you do it in just 30-seconds? What about 10-seconds?

You need to be able to spit out everything about your brand to a boss or networker in just seconds. If you can't capture their attention, they're going to move onto the next person in the room who can! No one wants to listen to a 60-second aside about a person and what makes them special. We want the summary and we want it to be cute, clever, and concise. I know you all agree with me!

How do you create your personal branded elevator pitch? Here are a few tips:

- **Keep It Brief:** Your personal brand pitch should be less than 30-seconds. You don't need to include your resume or overly promote yourself. Rather, the pitch should recap of who you are and what you do.

- **Add in Persuasion:** Naturally, if you are networking in an industry like accounting, you may need to add in a little creativity to keep the listener interested. Your speech should be compelling enough to spark the listener's interest in your idea. Mention something unique about your background, your experience, or what you do. If that's not interesting, talk about your passion for the industry. No one is ever going to turn an ear to passion.

- **Share Your Skills:** This is your time to mention your skillset. Try to focus on assets that add values to current requirements from these companies. Maybe accounting firms need well-traveled individuals today. Mention that you are a seasoned travel planner, etc.

- **Practice in the Mirror:** You don't have to test this speech out for the first time in a public forum. Why not say it to your mirror, your pet, or your mom? Practice your pitch over and over again so it doesn't make you nervous in person. People can tell if you are nervous – it will take away from your persuasion.

- **Be Positive and Agile:** No two settings are ever going to be the same. Read your audience. Are you talking to 80-year-olds or 13-year-olds? Be able to adjust and adapt your pitch depending on who is listening. Additionally, always be positive. Don't mention your dislike for something or your hatred for a previous job. Talk about positivity.

- **Close with Your Goals:** Recruiters want to know that you are passionate about this industry and here to stay. The best way to convince them of that is with a mention of your goals. Do you want to be part of this industry for the rest of your life? Do you want to change it for the better? Round out your elevator pitch talking about your goals, no matter how big they may be.

Once your elevator pitch is done, have those business cards available and at the ready. All of this will come together in one culmination of your personal brand: your appearance, your pitch, your cards, and your values. It will be incredibly hard for the listener to forget about you after that.

Additionally, don't be afraid to reinvent the wheel! You don't need your pitch to follow this structure word-for-word. The important thing to take away is that it needs to be engaging, authentic, brief, and captivating. Don't be afraid to embrace some humor, too!

Conclusion

And with that, you have officially completed our crash guide to building a personal brand that is effective, memorable, and unique to you. You can't afford to ignore your personal brand in a world where branding is paramount – thanks to coronavirus, it's only going to grow more in importance. Now is the time for you to accept that it's here. But, with our information and tips, you can use this personal branding to your advantage.

We are an academic community of experts, individuals, and researchers that want to help you be the best version of you. Too many students and graduate students assume they need to do all of this alone. That's just not true. We are here to be an expert resource for you and answer all of those pressing questions.

Don't forget to check out our information portals for all Honor Society members. We host a Vault.com portal that includes career, industry, and company research. It's a great way to kickstart your process in identifying the job that is perfect for you: https://www.honorsociety.org/benefits-coupons/career-insider-premium-access-over-100-industry-guides-and-5000-company-profiles.

Additionally, our Job Board Selection can be found here: https://jobs.honorsociety.org/.

If you have any questions about personal branding and the content of this book, please do not hesitate to reach out to us! We are a two-way communication channel here to help YOU!

www.ingramcontent.com/pod-product-compliance
Lightning Source LLC
Chambersburg PA
CBHW070518220526
45467CB00002B/728